THE 12 WORST **EARTHQUAKES OF ALL TIME**

by Susan E. Hamen

12 STORY LIBRARY

www.12StoryLibrary.com

12-Story Library is an imprint of Bookstaves.

Photographs ©: Department of Defense, cover, 1; Semnic/Shutterstock.com, 4; Pam Joy/Shutterstock.com, 5; US Navy/Jeffrey Russell, 6; Frans Delian/Shutterstock.com, 7; Chadwick, H.D./PD, 8; Belish/Shutterstock.com, 9; US Geological Survey, 10; Ericbronder/CC3.0, 11; NOAA/NGDC/Pierre St. Amand, 12; NOAA/NGDC/US Navy, 13; Public.Resource.Org/CC2.0, 14; Public.Resource.Org/CC2.0, 15; Vladimir Platonow/CC3.0, 16, 28; Senior Airman Tiffany Trojca/US Air Force, 17; NormanEinstein/CC3.0, 18; Victor Morozov/CC2.5, 19; Smallcreative/Shutterstock.com, 20, 29; Gurgen Bakhshetyan/Shutterstock.com, 20; Greg Webb/IAEA, 21; David Rydevik/PD, 22; Frans Delian/Shutterstock.com, 23; Department of Defense, 24; Everett Historical/Shutterstock.com, 25; Unknown/PD, 26; Angelo Giampiccolo/Shutterstock.com, 27

ISBN
978-1-63235-534-8 (hardcover)
978-1-63235-599-7 (paperback)
978-1-63235-653-6 (ebook)

Library of Congress Control Number: 2018945324

Printed in the United States of America
Mankato, MN
June 2018

About the Cover

Street collapse from the 1964 earthquake–caused landslide in Anchorage, Alaska.

12 STORY LIBRARY

Access free, up-to-date content on this topic plus a full digital version of this book. Scan the QR code on page 31 or use your school's login at 12StoryLibrary.com.

Table of Contents

1

Large Earthquake Shakes Alaska's Rat Islands

Alaska is the largest state by land area in the United States. It is bigger than Texas, California, and Montana combined. Alaska is also the most sparsely populated state. Much of it is covered in ice and snow. Harsh conditions keep many people away.

The Aleutian Islands lie off of Alaska's west coast. The region experienced a huge earthquake on February 4, 1965. The temblor measured 8.7 on the Richter scale. It is called the Rat Islands earthquake because it happened closest to that archipelago.

The earthquake was very large, but it did little damage. There were no buildings or people on the Rat Islands. Slight cracks formed in wooden buildings on nearby islands. Two bridges

Shifting of the earth's tectonic plates can cause large cracks in the ground.

Tsunami hazard zones are now identified in Alaska.

were destroyed. Some asphalt runways were damaged.

The shifting of the earth's tectonic plates caused a tsunami. This did more damage than the earthquake itself. Shemya Island experienced tsunami waves about 35 feet (10.7 m) high. Flooding occurred. Damage was worst on Amchitka Island. Property losses there totaled $10,000, or $78,000 in 2018 dollars.

WHY DO EARTHQUAKES HAPPEN?

Earthquakes occur when two large pieces of the earth's crust slip and move. These moving pieces are called tectonic plates. The movement causes shock waves. They make the earth's surface shake. This shaking is what we call an earthquake. Smaller movements before and after an earthquake are called foreshocks and aftershocks.

0

Deaths reported from this large earthquake.

- The earthquake did little damage because of its remote location.
- The temblor measured 8.7 on the Richter scale.
- Tsunami waves caused more damage than the earthquake.

2

Indonesian Islands Devastated by Powerful Temblor

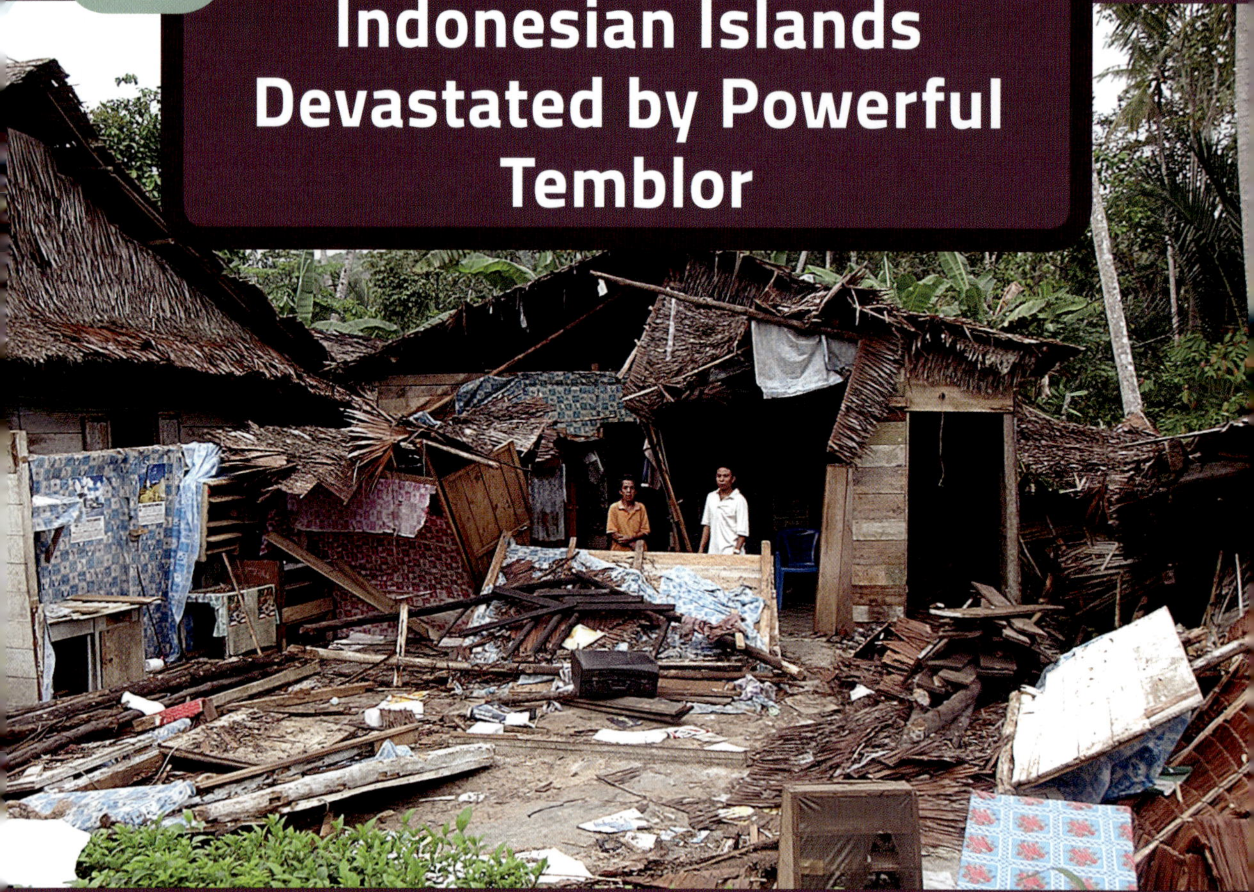

When disaster struck on the Indonesian islands of Nias and Simeulue, many people were already tucked into bed. At 11:09 p.m. on the night of March 28, 2005, an earthquake took place underwater. The quake measured 8.7 on the Richter scale. Islanders jumped up and ran for safety.

The people had reason to be afraid. A deadly earthquake had hit months before. That temblor caused a tsunami. An estimated 280,000 people in 11 countries died. The people of Nias and Simeulue feared another tsunami.

As people fled, fires broke out. Nearly 70 percent of buildings in the

2

Minutes the earthquake lasted.

- The quake measured 8.7 on the Richter scale.
- Nearly 70 percent of buildings in the Nias capital Gunungsitoli were destroyed.
- People worried a tsunami would hit the islands.
- Aftershocks hours after the quake worried islanders.

DOUBLING THE DAMAGE

Earthquakes can cause massive destruction. But often the tsunamis they create cause even more damage. Tsunamis are giant waves created by earthquakes or volcanic eruptions under the sea. A tsunami wave starts out small. But as it travels closer to land, it builds. Some tsunami waves are many stories high. They can wipe out entire towns.

Nias capital Gunungsitoli were destroyed. People were buried under debris. There was no power. Rescuers struggled to save victims. Many people pulled from the wreckage were dead. Aftershocks followed the earthquake. People on Nias, Simeulue, and nearby islands were afraid to stay home. They worried another quake or a tsunami would come. About 1,000 people died. Tens of thousands lost their homes.

The tsunami stranded this ship on top of a building.

3 Quake and Fire Nearly Destroy San Francisco

In 1906, San Francisco was growing. Nearly 400,000 people lived in the city. Many had come there with dreams of a better life. But on April 18, 1906, they awakened to a nightmare.

Just after 5:00 a.m., a 7.8 magnitude earthquake struck. Its epicenter was very close. There was a tremendous roar when it hit. Cracks opened in the streets. Buildings toppled. Gas lines were broken. Fires started. The quake also destroyed water mains. Firefighters connected hoses to hydrants, but no water came out. The fires burned for three days. Finally rain put them out.

About 28,000 buildings were leveled. More than 3,000 residents died. Another 250,000 people were left

The Mission District burning after the earthquake.

Seismographs record seismic waves, or vibrations, on paper.

homeless. The Great San Francisco Earthquake destroyed nearly 80 percent of the city. It caused damages of $500 million, or $13 billion in 2018 dollars. The earthquake is still considered one of the worst natural disasters in US history.

HOW ARE QUAKES MEASURED?

The magnitude of an earthquake equals the energy released at its source. Magnitude is measured with a seismograph. This tool uses zigzag lines to show a quake's seismic waves, or vibrations. Scientists use seismograph readings to learn the strength of earthquakes. Quakes are assigned a number between 0 and 10 on the Richter scale. The closer to ten, the more powerful the quake.

500

Number of city blocks completely destroyed.

- The earthquake had a magnitude of 7.8.
- Broken gas lines caused fires that roared through the city.
- Nearly 80 percent of the city of San Francisco was completely destroyed.

4

Peru's Worst Natural Disaster Buries a Town

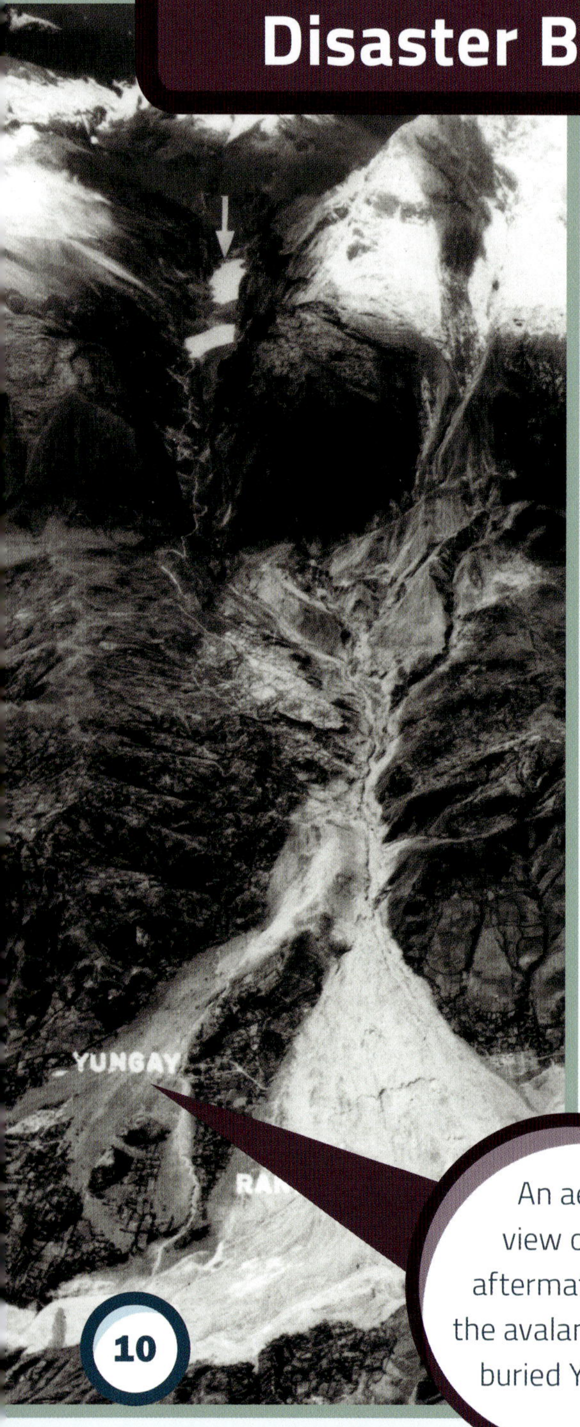

An aerial view of the aftermath from the avalanche that buried Yungay.

May 31, 1970, in Yungay, Peru started off as a relaxing Sunday. The first game of the World Cup was being broadcast. As adults listened to their radios, about 300 children crowded into a local stadium. They went there to watch a circus. It was an afternoon of planned fun for the town of nearly 25,000 people.

But at 3:23 p.m., disaster struck. An undersea earthquake in the Pacific Ocean off the coast of Peru shook the ground. The quake lasted only 45 seconds. But it measured a magnitude of 8.0 on the Richter scale. Homes, bridges, roads, and schools crumbled from the strong vibrations. The shaking also triggered a devastating avalanche. Ice, snow, and rock came racing down at 120 miles per hour (193 km/h). Within minutes, Yungay was buried.

400

Number of miles the quake could be felt throughout Peru.

- The earthquake lasted 45 seconds.
- An avalanche of ice, snow, and rock buried Yungay.
- An estimated 74,000 people died throughout Peru.

THINK ABOUT IT

After the disaster, the government of Peru would not allow the city of Yungay to be excavated. Instead, they declared it a national cemetery. Do you think people should remember places where tragedies happen? Why or why not?

The children rushed from the stadium, which was located out of the path of the avalanche. They looked at the town. Their homes had disappeared under 20 feet of mud, rock, and debris. Their mothers, fathers, and other family members were dead. In just a few minutes, all the children had become orphans.

Nearly 20,000 of Yungay's residents were killed that day. Throughout Peru, an estimated 74,000 people died. Communication systems were destroyed. More than a million people were left homeless. The Great Peruvian Earthquake is the worst natural disaster to ever hit Peru.

The entire town of Yungay was declared a national cemetery.

5 Chile Hit by Largest Quake in Recorded History

The most powerful earthquake ever recorded happened on May 22, 1960. The Great Chilean Earthquake had a magnitude of at least 9.5. It was so powerful it moved one town about 30 feet (9.1 m) to the west. Chile's land area expanded. The country was larger by about 1,500 football fields after the temblor.

Streets sank when the fault line ruptured.

A fault line more than 600 miles long (965.6 km) ruptured. That caused the ground to open up. Entire towns crumbled. But the devastation didn't stop there. Fifteen minutes after the quake, a tsunami hit the Chilean coastline. Waves rose nearly 80 feet (25 m) in the air. Then they crashed down on land. Thousands of buildings were destroyed. Two million people lost their homes. About 1,600 people died. Another 3,000 were injured.

Fifteen hours later, tsunami waves smashed into Hawaii, more than 6,600 miles (10,621 km) away. The waves reached nearly 35 feet (11 m). The tsunami killed 61 Hawaiians. Waves also hit the Japanese island of Honshu. There they reached about 18 feet (5.5 m). At least 1,600 homes were destroyed. Nearly 200 people died.

View after the tsunami hit Hilo, the most damaged city in the Hawaiian Islands.

$550 million

Amount of damage caused by the earthquake ($4.6 billion in 2018 dollars).

- The quake measured 9.5 on the Richter scale.
- One Chilean town was moved 30 feet (9.1 m) to the west.
- The temblor triggered tsunamis in Chile, Hawaii, and Japan.

A SHIFT IN EARTH'S AXIS

Some earthquakes have long-lasting effects on the earth. The Great Chilean Earthquake was so powerful that it shifted Earth's axis. The rotation of the planet was affected. Days became a few milliseconds shorter. Scientists have discovered that other earthquakes measuring 9.0 or greater have also shifted Earth's axis.

6 Quake Overpowers India on Independence Day

On August 15, 1950, people in India were preparing to celebrate. It was their Independence Day. Parties and feasts were planned. But at 7:40 p.m., joy turned to terror. A giant earthquake struck. Instead of celebrating, people were fighting for survival.

The 8.6 magnitude temblor affected other countries, too. The epicenter was in the town of Rami in eastern Tibet. China, East Pakistan, and Burma also felt the impact. But most of the damage occurred in India.

There, landslides blocked tributaries flowing down the mountains into the Brahmaputra River. When the water finally burst through the dirt, it caused a wall of water 30 feet high (9.1 m) to rush down the mountainside. Roaring floods charged through the Assam Valley below. Entire villages were washed

A town in Assam was submerged by the flooding.

An aerial view of Assam Valley farmland underwater.

away. Fields were destroyed. Farm animals and even elephants floated in the raging waters. Roads, bridges, and railroad lines were ruined.

The earthquake destroyed more than 2,000 homes, temples, and mosques. The death toll reached an estimated 1,500. The quake was the tenth-largest of the twentieth century.

70

Number of villages wiped out by the earthquake and flooding.

- The epicenter of the earthquake was in Rami, Tibet.
- The quake was felt in several countries, but most of the damage was in India.
- It was the tenth-largest temblor of the twentieth century.

THINK ABOUT IT

The Assam Valley was an agricultural area of India. The river flooding wiped out many of the crops planted. What hardships might this have caused?

7

Early Morning Temblor Rocks Chile

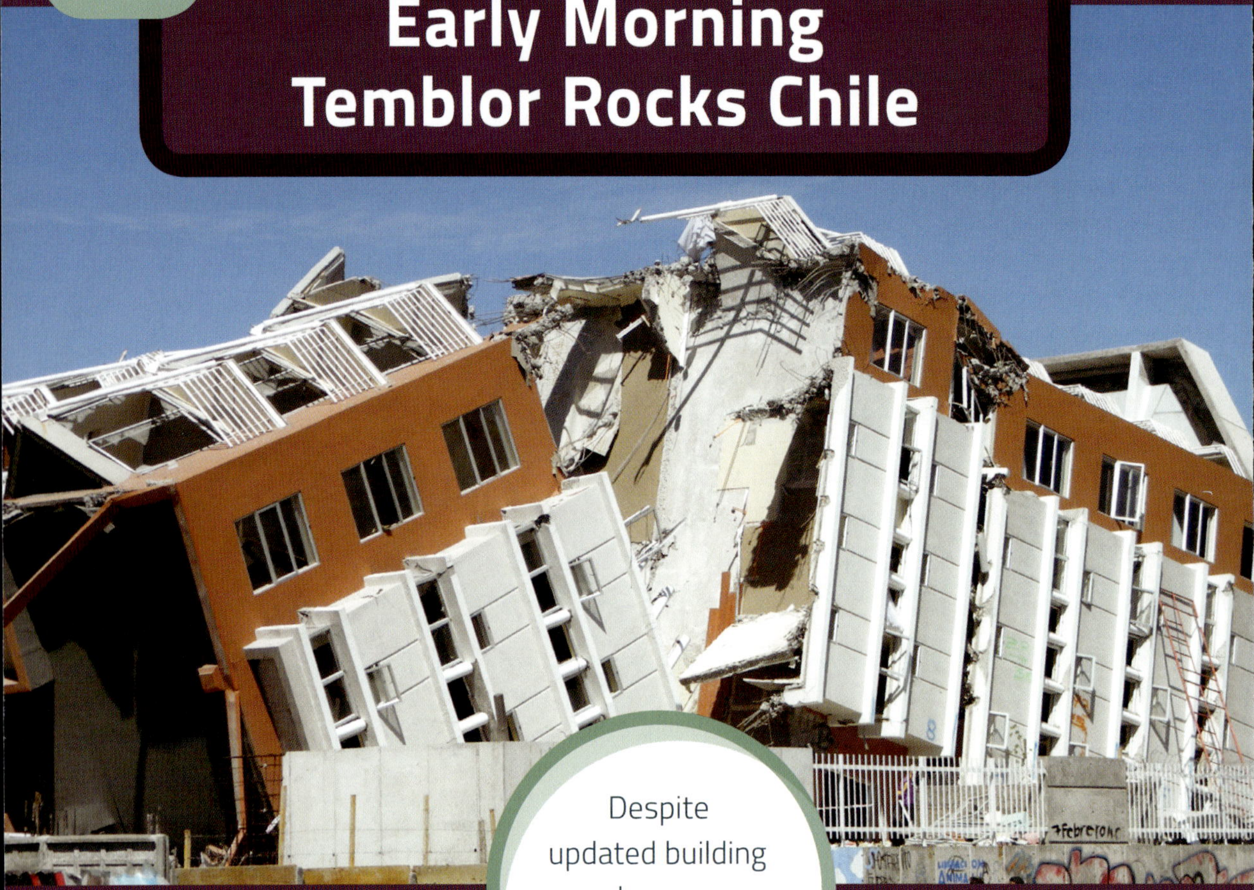

Despite updated building codes, many buildings were destroyed.

In the early hours of February 27, 2010, residents of Santiago, Chile awoke in terror. The earth was shaking. Cracks formed in the walls of homes. Ceilings collapsed.

An 8.8 magnitude earthquake was responsible. Its epicenter was about 200 miles (325 km) south of Santiago. A rupture along a fault line produced the temblor 22 miles (35 km) below the earth's surface.

The quake cut off power to many parts of the city. Water lines were broken. Buildings and bridges fell. Residents panicked as aftershocks began to occur.

800,000

Number of Chileans who lost their homes in the earthquake.

- The 8.8 magnitude earthquake struck Chile on February 27, 2010.
- Many residents of Santiago were left without power or fresh water.
- The earthquake produced tsunamis that reached California, Hawaii, and Japan.
- An estimated $30 billion in damage was caused by the temblor.

Hospitals struggled to help patients hurt in the strong quake. All day long, police and ambulance sirens blared through the city. That night, frightened citizens fought to get water, food, and supplies. Some people broke into stores and looted them.

The earthquake triggered a tsunami that devastated coastal areas of Chile. The town of Constitución was pounded by 50-foot (15-m) waves. Tsunami waves traveled across the Pacific Ocean, reaching California, Hawaii, and Japan.

The earthquake caused an estimated $30 billion in damages. Nearly 500 people were killed in the quake and tsunamis that followed. Hundreds of thousands of Chileans had their homes destroyed.

Field hospitals were set up to care for those hurt in the quake.

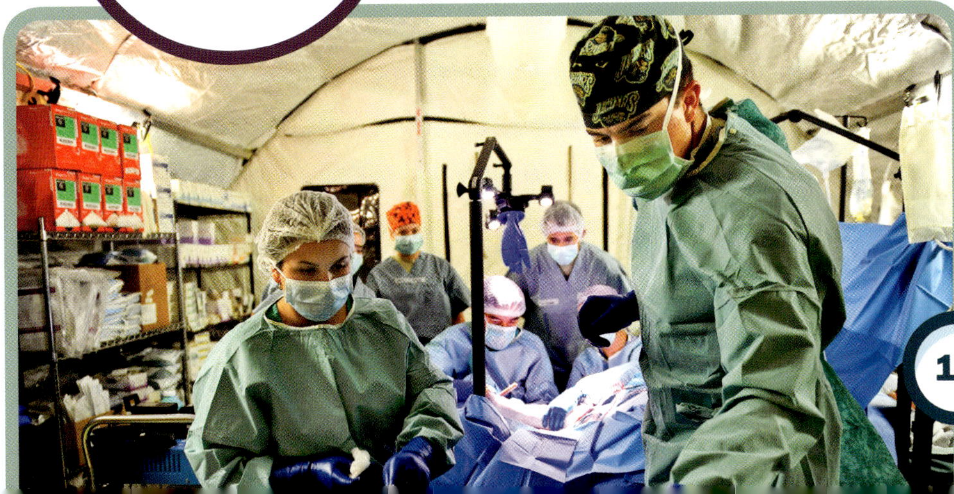

8

9.0 Earthquake Recorded in Kamchatka, Russia

On the Kamchatka Peninsula in Russia, powerful subduction earthquakes are common. One quake on November 4, 1952, made history. It was the first recorded 9.0 magnitude quake. The epicenter was in the Pacific Ocean east of the peninsula. People knew a tsunami would follow.

Immediately, police and rescue workers began preparing. Careful calculations told them they could expect the first tsunami waves about seven hours after the quake. The people of the Kamchatka Peninsula prepared for the worst.

Waves 50 feet (15.2 m) high pounded the shores of the peninsula. The small Kuril Islands to the south were also hit hard. Between 10,000 and 15,000 people

Map showing the direction of the tsunami that hit the Kuril Islands and Kamchatka Peninsula.

Severo-Kurilsk before the 1952 tsunami. The town was rebuilt at a higher level.

died on Kamchatka and the Kuril Islands.

Tsunami waves rippled far beyond Kamchatka. They reached the shores of Peru, Chile, and New Zealand. The Hawaiian Islands were badly damaged. Ocean water collided into boats and boathouses. Piers and roads were destroyed. A cement barge in Honolulu Harbor was hurled into a freighter. The waves did not lead to any deaths in Hawaii. But they did cause $17 million ($160 million in 2018 dollars) in damage.

350

Length in miles (563 km) of the subduction zone fracture in the Kamchatka region.

- The 1952 Kamchatka earthquake was the first 9.0 magnitude earthquake ever recorded.
- Deadly tsunami waves hit the Kamchatka Peninsula and the Kuril Islands.
- The earthquake took the lives of between 10,000 and 15,000 people.
- On the Hawaiian Islands, tsunami waves caused property damage.

DEADLY WAVES MAKE SHORE

Three waves between 50 and 60 feet (15.2 and 18.2 m) hit the shores of Severo-Kurilsk in Russia. Many of the townspeople fled to higher ground after the first wave. But most returned to town. They did not expect any more waves. When the second wave hit, over one-third of the residents drowned.

9

Japan's Largest Earthquake Causes Nuclear Meltdown

It was a Friday afternoon in the coastal town of Namie, Japan. Workers looked forward to weekend fun.

Those plans changed at 2:46 p.m. That's when a 9.0 magnitude earthquake struck off the coast. Its epicenter was about 80 miles away, on a thin strip of ocean crust.

Disaster officials knew a tsunami would probably follow. Workers who lived close to the ocean were ordered to go home. They were told to help evacuate elderly residents to safety. When the tsunami arrived, it looked like smoke rolling over the trees. Some people thought it might be a fire. But what looked like smoke was the spray of the tsunami wave. Soon after, waves began pummeling Namie. Houses filled with water and burst open. People were swept away in the rushing water. Many

An estimated 70 percent of the debris swept into the ocean sank to the sea floor.

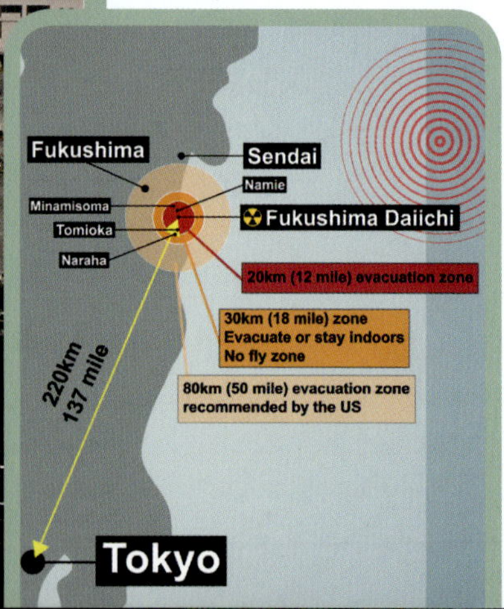

drowned. Others were hurt by debris in the water. In total, there were an estimated 22,000 fatalities.

The March 11, 2011 earthquake was the largest ever recorded in Japan. In addition to triggering a tsunami, it damaged reactors at the Fukushima nuclear power plant. This caused explosions and radiation leaks. Radiation can be deadly to humans. The area around the plant was unsafe for people to return to after the tsunami.

The Japanese earthquake caused $300 billion in damage. Six years later, in 2017, 50,000 people were still living in temporary housing.

5 million

Tons of debris swept into the ocean following the tsunami.

- A 9.0 magnitude earthquake struck off the coast of Japan.
- About 22,000 people lost their lives in the quake and the tsunami that followed.
- The 2011 earthquake near Namie was the largest ever recorded in Japan.
- Damage to nuclear reactors caused fiery explosions and dangerous radiation leaks.

Inspectors continue to monitor the decommissioning of the damaged power plant today.

10

Quake Off Sumatra Coast Is Deadliest in History

Most people had no warning the tsunami was coming.

1.7 million

Number of people left homeless after the earthquake and tsunami.

- The quake lasted about 10 minutes.
- It measured at 9.1 on the Richter scale.
- It caused more deaths than any other earthquake in history.
- The tsunami that followed caused damage in 14 countries.

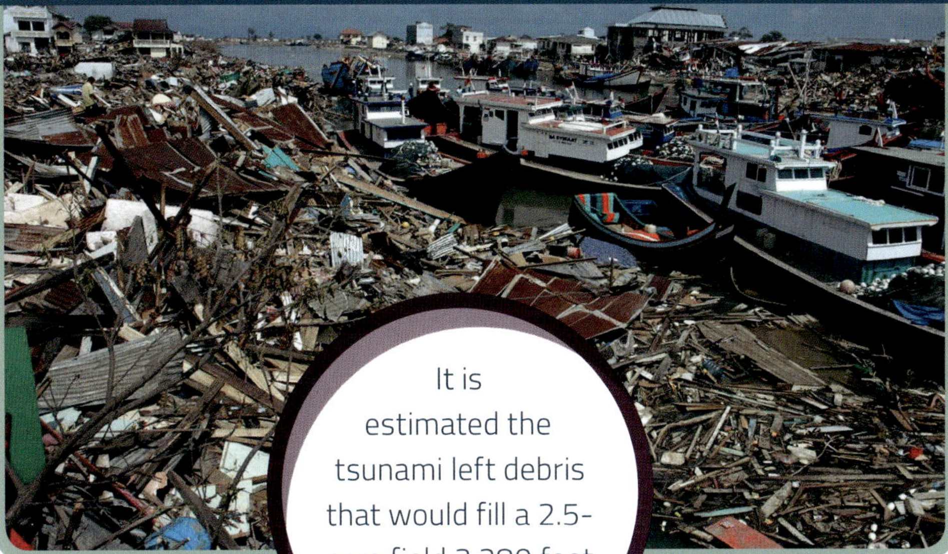

It is estimated the tsunami left debris that would fill a 2.5-acre field 3,280 feet high (1,000 m).

Most earthquakes last less than a minute. But on December 26, 2004, a 9.1 magnitude quake lasting more than 10 minutes struck off the coast of Sumatra.

In nearby Thailand, the day began with blue skies. Tourists kayaked and played on the beach in the morning sun. But at 7:59 a.m., something happened. Some survivors remembered that the air didn't feel right. They looked out to sea. A large wave was approaching. But it wasn't a normal one. It was a tsunami wave. The wall of water crashed down on the tourists. People were swept up in the roaring water, along with debris.

Thailand was not the only nation hit by deadly waves from the quake. Tsunami waves spread across the Indian Ocean, affecting 14 countries. They reached 30 feet (9 m), causing great destruction. More than 225,000 people died. Many thousands more were injured or missing. Indonesia, Sri Lanka, India, Maldives, and Thailand suffered the worst damage. Whole villages and towns were wiped away. Homes, buildings, businesses, and farms were destroyed.

The 2004 earthquake off the coast of Sumatra caused more casualties than any other earthquake in recorded history. Included among the dead were many tourists visiting the region.

11 The Great Alaska Earthquake Shakes the North

Damage along the coast was extensive.

The day was March 27, 1964. People in Anchorage, Alaska, were settling in at home for the evening. At 5:36 p.m., the ground began to shake. Most adults knew it was an earthquake. But no one imagined the damage it would cause.

THINK ABOUT IT

When the powerful earthquake struck, families scrambled to get out of their houses. Why do you think they fled their homes? Where might they go?

200

Height in feet (60 m) of the Alaska earthquake's largest tsunami wave.

- The earthquake destroyed much of Anchorage, Alaska.
- A tsunami caused damage on the Alaska and California coasts.
- The 9.2 magnitude quake lasted for five minutes.

Houses shook and rolled like boats on a stormy sea. Dishes, canned foods, and containers flew from cupboards and crashed to the floor. Furniture tipped over. People struggled to get out of their homes.

Outside, telephone poles swayed. Cars shook and bumped into each other. Deep cracks opened in the ground. People scrambled to avoid being swallowed up by the large holes. City water and sewer pipes were broken. So were gas and electrical lines.

A tsunami caused added destruction on Alaska's coast. Many of the towns along the coast of Prince William Sound and Kodiak Island were swept away. California was also hit hard with 12 deaths and millions of dollars in damage. Waves swept across the Pacific Ocean and reached Hawaii and Japan.

The Great Alaska Earthquake of 1964 was a magnitude 9.2 quake. The ground shook for five minutes. More land shifted and moved than in any earthquake previously recorded. The quake took the lives of 131 people. It did nearly $311 million in damage ($2.5 billion in 2018 dollars). It remains the strongest earthquake ever recorded in North America.

The town of Seward had some of the worst destruction.

12 Italian Earthquake Survivors Struggle to Rebuild

On January 11, 1693, a 7.4 magnitude earthquake struck Sicily, Calabria, and Matta in southern Italy. Shortly after the quake, residents saw the seawater withdraw. In the town of Augusta, ships in the harbor rested on a waterless sea floor.

A copper engraving from 1696 depicts the extensive damage to the city of Catania.

But the water was not gone. It came thundering back in a large tsunami wave. The tsunami destroyed at least 45 cities in Italy. More than 60,000 people died.

The ancient city of Catania lost two-thirds of its population. In the days following the earthquake and tsunami, there was chaos in the city. Survivors fought for food and supplies. Some people thought Catania was too badly damaged to rebuild. Nearly every building had been destroyed. Feeling helpless, many survivors fled the city.

With the help of officials from neighboring regions, Catania began to rebuild. Citizens set up temporary shelters outside the city walls. Over the next several years, rubble was cleared away.

The portal from St. George Cathedral, in Ragusa, Sicily, is all that remained of the building after the earthquake. It still stands today.

SAFER STREET CONSTRUCTION

Before the earthquake, Catania's city streets were narrow. This led to the deaths of many citizens. People trying to flee were hurt by collapsing buildings during the quake. During the rebuilding of Catania, city streets were made wider. This would allow for safer evacuation if the city ever had another earthquake.

New homes, buildings, and churches were constructed. Today Catania is the second-largest city in Sicily.

80

Approximate number of years it took to rebuild Catania.

- The 7.4 magnitude earthquake struck Italy in 1693.
- A tsunami destroyed 45 towns, including Catania.
- Temporary shelters gave the people of Catania a place to live during reconstruction.
- Catania is an important city in Southern Italy today.

Staying Safe If There Is an Earthquake

- Before an earthquake occurs, have a disaster plan ready. Know where the safest spots are in every room of your home.

- If an earthquake strikes, take shelter under a heavy piece of furniture, like a desk or table. This can help protect you from falling objects in your home.

- Remember Drop, Cover, and Hold On! Drop under a table or desk, cover your eyes to protect them, and hold on until the earthquake stops.

- Stay indoors until the shaking stops. Moving can put you at risk of being hurt by falling debris.

- Stay away from windows. Breaking glass can cause serious injury.

- If you're in bed when the earthquake starts, place a pillow over your head. It can help protect you from falling objects.
- If you are outdoors when the earthquake starts, move away from power lines and tall trees. Stay away from anything that might fall on you and hurt you.
- Once the earthquake stops, check for injuries. Be careful to avoid fires or deep cracks in the ground.
- Expect aftershocks. If you feel more shaking, Drop, Cover, and Hold On!

Glossary

archipelago
A group of islands.

crust
The outer layer of the earth.

epicenter
The point on the earth right above where an earthquake begins.

fatalities
Deaths occurring from disease or disaster.

fault line
A long crack in the earth's surface where earthquakes usually occur.

loot
To steal goods or property, especially during war or a crisis.

mosque
A Muslim place of worship.

peninsula
A piece of land sticking out from a larger area of land that is almost completely surrounded by water.

Richter scale
A system used to measure the strength of an earthquake.

shock waves
Seismic waves that spread through rock in all directions during an earthquake.

subduction
When one tectonic plate moves under another one, often causing an earthquake.

tectonic plates
Layers of the earth's crust that move and sometimes fracture.

temblor
An earthquake.

tsunami
A large ocean wave that is caused by an undersea earthquake.

For More Information

Books

Anniss, Matt. *The Science of Earthquakes.* New York: Gareth Stevens, 2013.

Furgang, Kathy. *Everything Volcanoes and Earthquakes.* Washington, DC: National Geographic Society, 2013.

Owens, Meredith P. *Earthquakes.* New York: PowerKids, 2017.

Index

About the Author

Susan E. Hamen has written more than 30 books for children on various topics including the Wright brothers, World War II, and ancient Rome. Hamen lives in Minnesota with her husband, daughter, and son.